The Weather
SUNSHINE

Terry Jennings

Chrysalis Children's Books

First published in the UK in 2004 by

Chrysalis Children's Books

An imprint of Chrysalis Books Group PLC

The Chrysalis Building, Bramley Road, London W10 6SP

ISBN 1 84458 069 5

British Library Cataloguing in Publication Data
for this book is available from the British Library.

Produced by Bender Richardson White

Editorial Manager: Joyce Bentley
Project Editors: Lionel Bender and Clare Lewis
Designer: Ben White
Production: Kim Richardson
Picture Researcher: Cathy Stastny
Cover Make-up: Mike Pilley, Radius

Printed in China

10 9 8 7 6 5 4 3 2 1

Words in **bold** can be found in New words on page 31.

Picture credits and copyrights
Corbis Images Inc.: cover (Richard Clune) and page 16. Digital Vision Inc.: pages 4, 7, 8, 12, 13.
Ecoscene: pages 10 (Chinch Gryniewicz), 18 (Nick Hawkes), 19 (Christine Osborne), 23 (Martin
Jones), 28 (Angela Hampton), 29 (Tony Page). PhotoDisc Inc.: pages 1 (Andrew Ward), 2, 5 (Jeremy
Woodhouse), 17 (Andrew Ward/Life File), 20, 24 (Glen Allison), 25 (Emma Lee/Life File). Rex
Features Ltd.: page 27 (Travel Library). Steve Gorton: pages 6, 9, 11, 22. Terry Jennings: pages 14, 15,
21, 26.

Contents

About the sun

The **sun** is a huge ball of burning **gases** far off in space. The sun is much bigger than our earth.

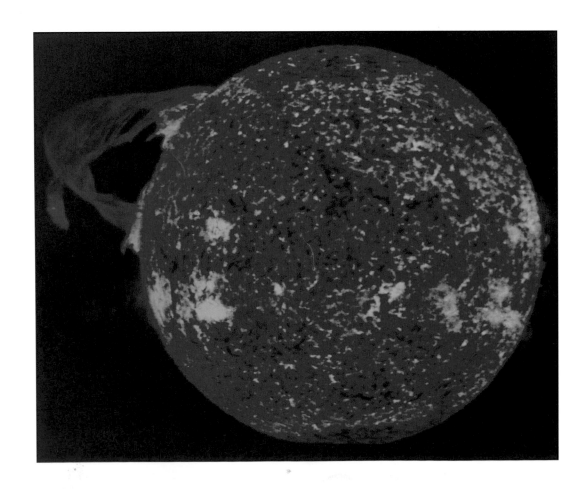

The sun looks small because
it is a long way away.

Never look straight at the sun.
It will damage your eyes.

Sunlight

Early in the morning, the sun begins to appear. We call it **sunrise**.

During the day, the sun gives us **light**. Even when the **clouds** cover the sun, we get its light.

Making shadows

If something gets in the way of **sunlight**, it makes a **shadow**. A shadow is the same shape as the thing that made it.

Shadows move during the day as our earth turns in the sky.

Darkness

At night, when we can no longer see the sun, it gets **dark**. Only a little light comes from the moon and stars.

At night, electric
lights help us to see.

Heat from the sun

The sun gives us **heat**. It is fun to play outside on a warm, sunny day.

The sun gives us most heat during summer. Some animals like to lie in the sun.

Sun and plants

Plants use sunlight to help make their food. Plants catch the sunlight with their leaves.

If plants are grown in the dark, they look yellow and weak.

Towards the light

Plants grow upwards towards the sun. The leaves of these trees are bunched at the top to get the most sunlight.

Some flowers, such as this sunflower, always face the sun to catch its light and heat.

Using sunlight

This calculator works using sunlight. The black strip at the top is called a **solar** panel. It changes light into electricity.

The solar panel next to this
house uses sunlight to warm
water. People in the house
use the warm water to wash.

Telling the time

You can tell the time by the sun. **Sundials** like these can show the time on a sunny day.

A pointer leaves a shadow on the face of the dial. The dial is marked in hours like a clock.

MY TIME IS IN THY HAND

LET OTHERS TELL OF STORMS AND SHOWERS
I'LL ONLY COUNT YOUR SUNNY HOURS

Rainbows

Sunlight is made up of lots of different colours. A **rainbow** is made when the sun shines through raindrops.

The raindrops split up the sunlight into seven different colours, from red to violet.

Sunsets

At the end of the day, the sun sinks lower and lower in the sky. This is called a **sunset**.

As the sun sets, it often makes beautiful colours in the sky.

Sunbathing

The heat from the sun can dry the soil so that it cracks.

If we stay out in the sun too long, it can dry and burn our skin. This makes us red and sore.

Safe in the sun

We use sun cream to stop sunlight harming our skin.

Wearing a sun hat keeps your head cool. Sunglasses protect your eyes from sunlight.

Quiz

1 What is the sun made of?

2 What do we call it when the sun first appears in the morning?

3 Can you see the sun in the sky at night?

4 What is made when something blocks the sunlight?

5 What colour are plants that are grown in the dark?

6 When can we tell the time with a sundial?

7 What does a solar panel do?

8 What can you do to stop your skin getting burned by the sun?

The answers are all in this book!

New words

cloud a mass of tiny water drops, smoke or dust floating in the air.

dark with little light.

gas any air-like substance: you cannot see or feel most gases.

heat warmth; the pleasant feeling we get from the sun, a fire or a radiator.

light something that shines to help you see things.

rainbow the curve of many colours we see in the sky when sun shines through rain.

shadow the dark shape formed by something that gets in the way of sunlight.

solar a word describing something to do with the sun.

sun the star we see in the sky during the day.

sunbathe to sit or lie in the sun.

sundial a device that shows the time by a shadow made by the sun.

sunlight the light from the sun.

sunrise the time in the morning when the sun first appears in the sky

sunset the time in the evening when the sun is going out of sight.

Index